Existential Cowboy

Existential Cowboy

Brian
R.
Strauss

Chula Vista, California

Cover Art by Elsa Muñoz
Author Photo by Joshuat Nava
Cover Design by Rachel Taylor

Any poem told from the first-person perspective is not the author, but a fabricated narrator for the purpose of the poem.

No artificial intelligence (AI) was used in the making of any part of this book.

First Edition.

A **SWOLLEN APPENDICES** Publication

978-0-9963221-4-0

Acknowledgments

To my most incandescent love – mother to our sons (cats) – you are my peace, thank you for always supporting my passions and for making our home a most comforting, peaceful, and loving space. My love for you is immeasurable and I'm so glad after all these years we finally made it happen. Te quiero mucho.

To my feline sons, Rogelito and Benito – finding you each were total accidents, I had no idea how to take care of a cat when I found [Ro], but we figured it out together and then your brother Benito somehow found us in that Sprouts parking lot on third avenue. You're good boys. You consistently slow my writing progress though.

Thank you to both Briana Muñoz and Ryan Bradford who have both been kind enough to read and provide blurbs for *Existential Cowboy* as well as previously for *Call of the Void.* I have a deep deep respect for the work you both do as artists and for the local artistic community as a whole.

Huge thank you to Elsa Muñoz for contributing her painting "Sol Partiendo el Humo" for use in the cover design at no cost because in her words, "I don't charge–we gotta look out for each other." Your kindness is something I'll do my best to pay forward.

Thank you to Karla Cordero for writing a blurb despite her crazy schedule. To have the words of such an exceptional poet like yourself on my book is a great gift and it does not escape me.

Words About *Existential Cowboy*

'*Existential Cowboy* is a poetry collection where no object, movement, or sound goes unnoticed. In this observational narrative, each poem zooms in and lingers on the complexities of love, landscape, and all that light touches. Strauss moves through his surroundings with a vulnerability that admits, "I think there's a lesson here, but I haven't figured it out," only to arrive at the harder wisdom that "all that was once beautiful has worn away to memories of something more beautiful." Here's what happens when we pay attention using the heart as our eyes." — Karla Cordero, author of *How To Pull Apart The Earth*

"Existential Cowboy unpretentiously romanticizes everything from the low-tone, bedroom conversation to the awkward mini-mart interaction while day-drinking. Read this book or else." — Briana Muñoz, Author of *Everything is Returned to the Soil*

"Brian Strauss' Existential Cowboy feels like a sea change of monumental proportions, a portrait of an artist coming into his prime. The whirlwind of emotions that defined earlier works like Strung Like Puppets and Call of the Void has been replaced with a laser beam: focused, intentional, and poignant.

There's a maturity here that feels earned in the hardest way possible, and melancholy drips from every page. But that's not to say Existential Cowboy is a downer. Rather, it's a hug. It's commiseration. These poems remind us that we reinvent ourselves many times throughout our lives, and every new iteration is simultaneously painful and beautiful." — Ryan Bradford, Founder of AwkSD

To H.Z.

The empty seat is for you.

I know you'd hate the attention, but your echoes live throughout these poems.

Poems

Eating Yellow Paint

I get so excited seeing the ocean
When it's been so long, I can breathe the saltwater breeze
And feel the rough sand being blown with that lovely coastal stench

As far as the sun is willing to travel, there are great luminous reflections
Delicately pulsing, small tears in the surface being torn and restitched
And torn again

The air here hangs differently
It meanders amid the fabrics of your clothes
And it dampens your hair in the chilly early mornings
Before the marine layer is burned away in the afternoons

From the window of my friend's apartment in Mission Hills
We can see the ocean sprawled across the horizon
The nearby downtown skyline its jewel,
A heart ready to be thrust into the depths and embraced

I would kiss the sky if I could,
With its painterly strokes

Broad and bright reds smeared like the drippings
Of a canvas being wiped from the blooming brush

My lips stained red with sky.

Ah, yes

If I could feel the textures of the clouds commingling brazenly
And the arched burst of the sun's final throes

I have been away for exactly one year
And I am more in love than I have ever been

On the grass near the botanical garden
Crowds of people walk through,
Many come to sit on their respective
Patches of grass and play Seurat

As though he might be perched just out of sight
Pecking away as the pointillists do,

Though he wasn't strictly pointed.

We've a bottle of wine tucked into our stitched canvas
Bag alongside some cucumber sandwiches, pieces of cheeses,
A dollar baguette we found at the supermarket while perusing
For goodies

The perfect bite, my friend says to herself
Lifting a trisket with the fixings to her mouth.

The three of us laugh and point
And I roll onto my side gripping my ribs in
Humorous agony

If only Van Gogh had known,
He only need eat cheese.

The Terrarium

On the dining room table
There is a small terrarium

At its center lay
Three eggs

Ensconced in a glass shell
Sleeping in a bed of
Pine needles

Stems of flowers
Growing from beneath eggs

Burgeoning maw
Gnashing floral teeth

Ovum peeled back
Transparent and gleaming

Black veins spread roots
Across the blooming gamete

Color fades from the eggs
Pulsing in brief sojourns
To other planes

Reprieve from reclamation
A hand lifts the glass-nippled lid

Vapors slowly pour out

Drops of colorless spectres
Drip from the glassy innards

Each a new inkling to be seeded
Blots that bleed through the bed
Of needles

Where in the dirt
New forms begin to shape life.

And each drop
Births new light.

The Last Time We Made Love

I've been thinking about you. I woke up this morning and remembered you were in my dream last night. Sometimes when I wake up, it feels more like a memory, and the longer I'm awake the farther I seem to get from it. We hadn't spoken in a while, but I called you to see if you wanted to grab dinner. You said you'd have to ask your boyfriend. Then there was another call and you said again you'd have to ask your boyfriend.

At dinner you were smiling like you didn't know why you were there, or at least you didn't know what to expect. You told me there was no point, that it was too late for us to be anything if there ever was a chance. You didn't touch your wine and I swallowed mine.

In bed I had my nose buried in your hair. You rolled over and there you were. Big brown eyes with a dumb sense of wonder about them. I was obsessed.

Your hair was matted across one side of your head and your face had small indentations from your pillow. I kissed the tip of your nose. You laughed and pushed me away. I pulled you closer,
Kissing your neck and under your chin, laughing with you until neither of us were laughing. Your hands slid up my neck, to my cheeks, and your fingers fit beneath my ears.

You pushed me onto my back and kissed down my chest, looking up at me and smiling before kissing further. Your soft hands slid up my hip and held my hand as I closed my eyes and tilted my head back.

You grabbed me and climbed on top, putting me in you and leaning forward, my arms wrapped around you, your breasts pressed against my chest, sweat beginning to puddle between us already. We laughed at the sound of lapping moisture between each tender thrust.

We held our mouths open, breathing each other, until you stopped just to look at me. We looked into each other and we could see that it was something even if just in that moment and it felt beautiful and sad at the same time.

You with your sense of hope and your heart so full of love and tender affection, your fleeting desire for domesticity, and your enduring delicate fingertips that could touch my skin as if it were cooling sunlight.

You rolling me over on top of you and crushing me between your muscular thighs and telling me to finish in you, pulling me in as closely as you could, even closer still, your insides begun to flow out over us just as I reached my peak.

My head was on your shoulder and you were stroking my hair, kissing my ear. I asked you to spend the night.

I have so much love for you, you told me.

And then you were gone.

Life Bleeds from Your Pores

In the mirror I can see small lines beginning to form
At the edges of my eyes and at the peaks of my
Rosy cheeks, flush from the years spent drinking
Bottles of red wine and tequila in single sittings
Tiny red spots clotted in my pores.

We'd be sitting at the bar after having taken a few
Shots and a beer or two at home
And then we'd ask for a beer and shot each time
Until we'd each stumble out of the bar

When your memory is just a series of smudged
Sketches burned in black charcoal
Smeared across the canvas of your mind
Where it lies to you the next morning

While in bed you can hear the fissures of
Your brain beginning to rupture
Spouting malevolent vapors that burst
Without prejudice

Occasionally there are tears
And your hair begins to fall out

You learn to quiet the mental whispers
After guzzling a few glasses of water

And a few shots of tequila you're back in the game
Dried out and your stomach is eating itself

Ten years in a blink
Full of so much without meaning

A life spent trying to destroy your consciousness
And now you get to look in the mirror every morning
With tired eyes while you rub anti-aging cream into
Your face and wash your body with fig wash after

Even your cherry tomato nose is looking less…cherry.

You exfoliate in the shower and finish with a
Cold blast to lock in moisture and close your pores,
In the hopes that maybe, just maybe,
You'll finally stop the bleeding.

In Downtown Chula Vista

Red wine is being poured from the glass chalice
Into a water-spotted glass

Cheap particle-board bench struggles
Beneath me with a tender groan

Outside it's bright and there are children
Playing tag while parents sip beer under canopies

I can hear passing cars   a honk in the distance
Sirens

There's a mirror propped against the wall
My smudged reflection - my ill-fitting shirt - my broad strands
Of black curls - my tan, oily, skin - damp glistening layer of sweat

There is no one else sitting, but
Employee behind the bar and one of the cooks
At table next to mine writing in her notebook

Breeze that drifts through window is chilly
So I throw a shawl over my shoulders

Music in the cafe is too loud,
At least they play good music

But the piano in the center of the room
Is too big for this small cafe

Owner is a broad shouldered man standing several inches
Taller than me, wearing a faded fedora, who talks too much
But is kind and means well

There is sincerity in the way he talks about his cafe
With excitement and endearment and I'm entertaining
His monologue, but god damn if I don't just want my
coffee

Beer is too expensive here, supposedly because it's imported
But twelve dollars for a big bottle still seems like too much
When I can get a sixteen oz pour down the road of some
local
Stuff for seven bucks

It's strange,
How the last time I'd been here, this street I mean,
It had been so different, so much less was here,
Back then it was just a place to lie on the grass
And read or listen to music on your headphones
Maybe have a picnic and sneak a joint in the parking garage

Now it's filled with all sorts of bars and breweries
New restaurants and cafes, dance halls for quinceañeras

A splendor of new places to drink eat and laugh amongst
friends
Because in this town, wherever you go there's a familiar face
Smiling back at you from behind the counter   sitting at a
nearby table

It's part of its charm   part of its nuisance.

In the evening the lowriders slowly skirt down the main drag
Bumping their loud stereos and raucous hydraulics
With bright colored lights, wearing plaid button downs
Reggaeton ringing out down the avenue

The sky glows with a fiery incandescence
Crashing waves of magma.

I'm smiling to myself as I walk.

I can smell the birria and adobada wafting through the air
From the food trucks
And the old Mexican men
With their button downs, wagging finger at los jovenes

Cálmense.

But they will do no such thing.

Car Wash Waiting Room

Waiting room sardined
broad man too large for his seat
An elderly Mexican woman on my other side

Ammonia and chlorine hangs in the air
Suspended in the fluorescent flourish of fixtures
That dimly flicker above us

My teeth feel sticky, forgot to brush them this morning.

I can see my car through the window
being pushed along conveyor track,

Young man in neon yellow vest
Points his power washer at windows then wheels.

He waves it down and waits for next car
Begins again.

I hear the pattering of water against the window.
Another car–another wash–another wave.

Squeak of rubber soles against linoleum tiles
Customer walks in looks around No
more seats
leans against vending machine
In hallway.

I see sweat stains expanding beneath gentleman's
Arms, just across from me.

He notices me looking   crosses his arms
Looks down at floor, forlorn expression.

My name is called out over the intercom, but
When I stand another man stands as well

I sit back down.

I'm sitting in a waiting room,
Behind the other customers there's a window
And I can see my car being pushed through.

I can hear the pattering of water against the window.
Another car–another wash–another wave.

The lights hum.

Elegy To a Marriage

peeling potato
Even though I prefer skin on

Water on stove slowly warms
Thin veneer of smoke coats
Kitchen from small bits of leftovers
Living beneath the burner

I chew on half a clove of raw garlic
Burns my tongue   my throat
There are tears in my eyes and I struggle
To speak momentarily

From the small bowl, my hand   a fingerful
Of diced onions and tomatoes

When's the last time we ate in?
Oh, it's been a while.

We should do this more often.
Mm, you know I hate cooking.

I know.

Cradled by the Ageless Orchestra

Alone at 3:30am
Resigned to consciousness
And quiet keystrokes of Satie

Gentle tapping of raindrops against bedroom window
Street lamps reflected in shallow pools of water

Splash of cars passing, lights flickering between blinds,
rays of light penetrate the darkness

Hungry and physically dilapidated, I have aged 5 years in
two
Beside me she is lying asleep or listening
to the same gentle rainfall

It'd be nice to have a cat.

In the living room a friend of roommate's snoring loudly
Sounds the way dogs do when they've had their vocal cords
cut out.

She and I laughed in bed about it
Loud enough for my roommate to ask the next
morning

What was so funny?

And now Satie is playing me through the eye of a pale blue
needle,
the punctured firmament recounting timeless divinity. He is

singing
sonnets with his fingertips. He is an old flower tucked
between the
pages of a book, dried up and beautiful.

Romantic, way one imagines drinking wine on a balcony
downtown,
overlooking urban starlights while Gymnopedies floats
across living
room, adrift in early morning air, in darkness of immutable
light.
Noble dawn always calling on us to receive it.

Nowhere is it ever described- but
it basks in itself as it awakens and as it lies down to sleep.

Every night and every morning,
Brown eyes beginning to glow like golden pools of dew

Until you've kissed sweet knuckles
In the palm of your hands
With all your delicate shapes.

Every Time I Hit a Bump

I hear a rattle in the back door
That makes me worry it's gonna pop open on the freeway
And all my shit's gonna fly out into the lane behind me

One time I was on the freeway and there was this truck
In its bed there were pieces of furniture stacked too high
High enough to sway when the truck would change lanes

And I was driving a different car then, a wide sedan that sat low to the ground
I didn't have the foresight at the time to see why it was unwise to drive
Behind that truck

Blasting down the 15 where it merges onto the 805 South
Wide turn, swing to the right- and off comes a stool

I felt my car crush its cheap construction, but I was worried my car was damaged
So I followed the truck and flashed my lights until we pulled over

He got out of his car and slowly stepped towards me
Long lugubrious steps until his sleepy eyes with their puffy eye-lids
Met mine

I ran over your stool.
Oh, alright. Your car looks fine.
Yeah, but can I get your info in case something turns up?

Just check it now.

I could feel myself grimace

I'd prefer to just get your info.
Take a look at your car and if there's an issue
we can work it out.

He was much taller than me and his face was weathered
from sun
His sweated black hair overgrowing from beneath his faded
hat as he wiped
His greasy forehead with his oil-stained t-shirt

I looked under my car as if I knew what I'd look for

Everything looks fine, I think.
Good.

We each got back into our cars
And I sat there thinking for a minute how much of my life
is eaten up by such stupid shit

I think there's a lesson here, but I haven't figured it out.

Smudge

In the living room where the blinds are shut
There's a strong odor of lavender doused carpet
With a dim candlelight tenderly illuminating your
Honey dipped eyes

Like staring into pools of marbled amber
You've chiseled the staggered features of my sur face
I am peeled back and away

And all that remained of me has dissolved

And you'll hold me from behind
Your arms wrapped around my neck and
Your lips against my cheek and
Your voice in my ear

Like some secret between us
The greatest inside joke
That only we're in on

Your eyeliner has smudged
Do I have raccoon eyes?
I smile and run my fingers through your
Jet black hair down your temples
Fibrous tesseracts brightly lit aflame
Upon your scalp the curled crown blooming
Vividly

Are you okay
Yes, are you

Ya

You seemed grumpy this morning
I could feel it in the kitchen
No not grumpy

It's okay to feel sad or grumpy
And not take care of everyone
You're human, it's okay to feel

No, not grumpy, sad.
I'm sad.
Not seeing every day is going to be hard.

I hope we get a repeat.

Silence.

Words never said.

Pomegranate

In a thick Eastern European accent
Waitress asked us what we'd like to drink

Four vodka flights, please.
Which flavors would you like?
Can we sort of divvy it up evenly so we've got two of every flavor?
Yes, that will be fine, we're just out of the horseradish flavor.
Damn! I love the horseradish blend.
My apologies, sir.
That's alright, we'll still do the flights. Thank you.

It wasn't long before she came back,
With a busser, each of them carrying a large wooden board
That held sixteen shots of vodka each, eight for each person.
The four of us thanked her and cheers'd our glasses

Can we start with the adjaruli? Do you have that tonight?
Yes, very good sir. I love that, one of my favorites.
The egg! I love the egg.
Yes, the egg is quite good with the cheese.
And the potato pierogies, could we also do an order of those?
Of course, sir.

I stood up to use the restroom,
They bring you your drink quick
To distract from how long it takes

To get your food, but

You know what you signed up for.

The walls are covered in writing
And the light dim,

Smell of roasted chakhokhbili
Wafts from the kitchen through the restaurant

In the dark hallway
Waiting for the restroom
I can see into the kitchen
Where they are roasting
Skewers of lamb over coals

I see a plate of beef stroganoff
Carried past me into the main dining room

A waiter squeezes by in the narrow hallway
Carrying a plate of chakapuli and smiling up at me
With a young anxious face

Restroom door opens.

At the table my friends are laughing over a joke
I missed and we are in love with our food
With the dim yellow light and with
Talking too loudly and smiling too broadly
And with our eager over-indulgences

It feels good to be surrounded with love.

We will finish our evening with a cup of espresso
And stumble out of the restaurant into the cold night air
Spitting pieces of coffee grinds onto the cracked
Evening sidewalk and saying

I love you
Before parting ways.

Box Truck

I circle the roundabout
At the entrance of the park

On the grass there's an elderly
Woman in a wheelchair
Someone in scrubs beside her

I pull my truck in
Way down at the end of the park
Away from the families playing frisbee on the grass
And the tan muscular men pulling their paddle boards
From the backs of their campers

Away from the police that
patrol the park's
Path

In the back of the truck
there are seven
small wooden boxes

Darkly lacquered with
Gold lock on the front

Matching gold plate on top
Each a different name
A different set of years

Some
Have a picture taped to the top

I take a screwdriver and pry the
Plates from the boxes

Each a casket for ashes
Small pieces of bone

From each box
I lift a plastic bag and set in
Brown paper bag

That's not something you just throw away.
Well what do we do with them then?
Just give them to me, I'll take care of it.
What are you gonna do?
I'll do something respectful. Probably better you know less, in case I get caught.

Across bright green grass
Under noon sun hanging at its highest point
Sweltering heat   sweat stains pool beneath
My arms and nape of my shirt

In my arms brown paper bag
With its rolled top

Small knife sticking out of my back
Pocket with its wooden hilt

Sunglasses fog

First steps on sand
From beneath my blurred lenses

I realize there's
A father watching his children play

Near water
Where algae has washed ashore

His eyebrows crawl towards his eyes
Where they try to look cavalier
Peripheral glance more noticeable
Than simply waving

Beneath bluff
Where grass ends

I pull each bag out.

Great puff of ash as
I slice my knife across plastic
Cloudy bursts on my shirt and pants

Shit - fuck fuck fuck

Bag wheezing out,
I swing my arms forward
Ashy ejaculate fires forth
In the water a gray cumulus that
Floats wistfully, if not stubbornly
Stationary

The more I look at it the more
It seemed to be waiting

For me or its friends
I don't know

Of course I was the holdup for their friends
So perhaps both

Covered in ash
I cut into another bag

I spill less
But I resign myself to ash and mud

It dawns on me,
Thinking of the father

That my appearance may give
a different impression

By third bag I can see bone fragments
Puncturing the cloudy grey veneer
That sloshes against the ashy shore

By end of seventh bag,
I'm sad

Someone had loved them enough to keep them
Long after they'd stopped sleeping at their feet

And now
I'm hoping there's a final wooden box
Without its stamped gold plate

No one left to add the name.

I toss my knife in the trashcan and wash my hands
In the park restroom,

Quickly for fear that someone might walk in

I take the boxes from my truck
Dump them in the trash can.

At the roundabout
Elderly woman was still sitting in her chair
Facing the ocean now, instead of the road

Her eyes empty
As if she saw nothing at all

I wondered
Who would roll me to the edge of the grass
When my mind was finally gone,

And who would sit with me
When I no longer knew they were there.

Little Vibrations Pulsing Through My Legs

On the table
Large glassy eyes with huge dilated pupils
Beautiful little black hole aperture
Framed in green

Small ears, one pointed upward
And the other a shriveled mass
Of scar tissue

I stroked my hand down his back to his butt
He raised his chin and his eyes widened
As I began to scratch under his chin

He stood up and threw himself
A breaching whale, thud of his body against wood
His primordial pouch stretched out beneath him

I held it in my hand then rubbed his chest and belly
He made biscuits in the air and purred

I looked into his sleepy eyes
And stroked his mackerel coat, thinking
How every time I see his beautiful face
Is like seeing him for the first time.

I put my hand on his paw
He pulled away and placed it on top of my hand.

Eyes delicately closed as he rested
His head in my lap.

Little vibrations
pulsing through my legs.

At The Gas Station

I refuse to put my hand on the pump

There's so many hands that must touch it each day
Hands that have been in too many places
But then   I've rarely seen a hand I didn't like

What about hands makes them good

Is it the lines?
The way some hands are thin with long bony fingers
And knuckles that seem to be trying to break from their
Fleshy prism

Or the way
Others are thick and stout
And calloused and weather worn
With small cuts of a workman's life

Maybe it's the way
Fingertips feel when they're just close enough
To graze the inside of your palm

Sensory anticipation

Perhaps
It's the cool delicate touch some hands have
That clasp yours gently as if to protect them
And soothe them

Or even

Infantile hands
Wrapping its entire hand around your one finger
With ungodly grip

How
A hand feels stroking your forehead
And running its fingers through your hair

And when
You feel the wrinkles carved into skin
You can read the lines of all the lives they've touched.

What about hands, says so much?

I'm stuffing mine into my pockets to dig for dollar bills
And only finding loose change, old receipts, and cigarette butts.

My hands are dirtied from the day spent digging up the garden
To plant new flowers for me to watch the birds and bees
Linger on their blossoming petals.

My hands hurt from the joints of my fingertips
Through the ball of my palm.

I finally begin to pump gas into my car,
An odd man waves.

I wave back unsmiling.

Between the Cracks in the Asphalt

Just over the gate at Bay Park the sun has already fallen
Below the crest of the cascading sand at Silver Strand
Smell of salty ocean air wafts through the
Narrow industrial streets

Families funnel out of the park
As the sun's warm glow begins to dissipate
Capitulating to evening ocean breeze

A block over there is the dull roar of engines
Humming in the yacht basin

As if the Earth had found its resonant frequency
For all that it contains

An elderly woman sits in her wheelchair near the road
With her nurse while they wait for the shuttle

Behind them on the grass there are a few lingering
Children tossing frisbee between each other

Small wakes splash against the shore
And reflect the last pangs of dimming sunlight
Hearkening for affection-

A siren for the sky betrothed to yearning.

Water from a leaking hydrant fills the cracks of the

pavement
Downstream it nourishes the small flowers beginning to bloom
From between the pieces of asphalt-

Cars drive over them indifferently, mechanically, and
They tremble with timid reticence, keeping to themselves
And clinging to their little spot in the world

A patch of grass to call your own
And a place to lay your head down
With a belly full of food
And just maybe someone to squeeze against

The sun is gone and the park is empty
And the little flower slumps in its damp soil.

The Celestial Incubus

It's 100 degrees outside
My bare, tanned, chest is wearing a thin veneer of sweat
And reflecting sunlight from between strands of black hair

I'm carrying bags in for myself
And the gaggle of women I've come with
All of whom are friends

Bags and bags of groceries
We spent a thousand dollars
At the Albertson's around the corner

Close enough that the next morning
When all of my cigarettes had gone
I'd be able to walk over to purchase
Two more packs while everyone napped

Just as we've finished unloading the cars
Of our luggage and our groceries

There's a knock on the front door
The owner whom we'd needlessly deal with

He's prattling on about the A/C and the noise
How important it is that we keep the noise down

Apparently you can't play music in Palm Springs
Which makes sense when you consider it's mostly
Elderly people, but less so in the case of just about everyone
else

Already there's been conflict
We'd made the one girl ride with the other girl
Because the last time I'd ridden with the one girl
She got blackout drunk on the drive off half a bottle
And I just don't have the energy in me for that sort of thing

Not even middle aged yet and I'm so tired all the time
Consumed by lethargy

The older I get   the more   disinterested
               I am
Quietly doing something very well in the comfort
Of   my living room
Is ample.

Truthfully I'd love to take up carpentry,
I've always been so envious of anyone
Who could work with their hands

To be able to build something
Piece it together

Or to craft something that no one sees but you
Your singular vision

By now the owner has finished his soliloquy
You're all grown so I know I don't have to tell you,

Except maybe him...he says pointing to me
He seems young.

I laugh and nod smilingly at him

Before walking him to the door

As my friends take care of putting away groceries
I go to the restroom to shit and change into swim shorts

Outside I light a cigarette   in the heat I can feel my skin
begin to warm
Mist sunscreen across my body and stand beneath the sun
Waiting for my skin to dry

Standing on the ledge near the hot tub, behind the house
you could
See in the distance not too far were the mountains

That's pretty…

I dip first my toe   warm   like bath water
I step down
Let myself gently fall beneath the surface

The silence that fills your ears when you float underwater
An enveloping hum- low and betrothed to nuance
Soaks you in   a celestial succubus
Everything that brings me pain stems from my yearning

All I can think about as the water flits between the strands
Of my floating hair is how much I ache

I ache with desire
I ache with loneliness
And I ache with regret

Every moment feels like a series of smeared thoughts

How white is supposed to represent all colors of the spectrum
And yet black is what you get when you actually mix it all together

Everything theoretical I try to love unequivocally
A failure of commitment was in giving me deliberation

But I'll kiss the sunset when I ride my bike down the wide
Residential streets in nothing but short-shorts and a flowery shirt
With long mismatch patterned socks and $15 huaraches

Sheltered from the light behind my thick rimmed
Spanish sunglasses with the tortoiseshell frame

Always on the edge of confession-

I keep reminding myself that it's okay to feel,
But I am too emotional to talk about it

Never did I want anyone to ever doubt how I felt about them
Even if it wasn't necessarily the truth

My friends inside,

Preparing snacks and drinks and playing music
And dancing and laughing   I feel a bit outside myself
So I sink back down until my ass touches the floor of the pool

And when I look up, the light bleeds through the glassy

surface
On my hands their stains glow with a cosmic ichor
My heart interrupts the dull hum of sensory deprivation
With a meandering pulse- dragging its tempo at a
languorous pace

What if I could hold my breath forever?

I don't know that I'd ever surface
If not for the face that looks down on me

A slender hand extending into the water
I grasp it between both my palms
And press it against my cheek
Close my eyes and kiss their fingers.

I still ache. But less so.

I Feel Veins Where Tears Carved Fissures in My Face

In dead space
where small pustules of oxygen wait to be inhaled–

–Distilled

where hair flees gravity stretching out every queer way
Like blooming moss depraved of moisture condensed and writhing inwardly
Drying and browning and flaking away in light tufts of once green follicles

Flesh a prism of ineptitude–of mortality–of
temptation– inebriation

And tombstones blow kisses from their pedestals of faith
Their grassy corsets punctured by flowers blooming from bodied kindling
An aviary borne of rib   caged– convex and mirrored
Stymied by throbbing organ– monument of ridicule to gynic flesh

Where bone marrow echoes solitude a rapture of cadavers
Rupturing flesh immersed and engraved– a smeared visage
Of coagulating blood, a vein meridian

The triage of verisimilitude relentless and unapologetic

I am become the earth He will say as he forages for

meaning
Affectionately touching cosmic druids– embers of star lit
aflame
A starry cosmesis of cartilage and debasement herniating
where
A gut once grew inexorably

Starvation cometh
Bloated with malnourishment,
She will gaze into her navel and
Scream

Oleander particles, like white phosphorus– silently bursting
Delicate glowing tendrils of white space dust
Carving fissures in eternity

A flesh wound of the soul
Cut into digestible bites
Meager and pathetic

Drunk and staring dead-eyed
String of drool
Slurringly,

What's wrong?

She slides closer, continually asking
With dim pupils, struggling to align, ravenous for affection
And I sliding away with a muscular tenseness
My bones stiffened and demurring

A picture of the evening measured in increments of howls
In cutaways of laughter punctured by tears

Where darkness of basement speakeasy cradles
Our group with loving arms and cruel kisses

In the mirror we are staring,
Fractals of light gliding over all

There is nowhere to do cocaine in private.

Restroom attendant pumps soap into my hands, standing nearby
Offering me a mint and a hand towel

Cigarettes are too expensive to purchase in the restroom
For what could be gotten between bars

Laughter–dancing–music
Lights are dimmed for performance

An absence of identity begins to percolate
In subdued light, halfway through performance
I have a glass of blanco tequila on ice with lime in my hand
He pulls me behind a pillar, his hands caressing my neck

There are memories of taste
Another bar, another night
Where people sing out of key without a sense of humor

Him holding me by the wrist, looking at me
With eyes larger than this stomach

My name– before he throws himself at me
His lips coagulating with mine
A long simmering tension being realized

His wife's a nice guy but he's a terrible person.

Is it too late in life to enjoy company?
His blonde hair bleached from our trip to Cabo San Lucas
Where he practiced his wedding speech

Where in the sun I lay drenched and bathed in luminescence
My flesh tanned subtle color of my mother
Her indigenous heart mingling with the affectations of assimilation
Hopes being dragged across concrete and viciously beaten to death

Lingering sensation of the facsimile of ethnic pride
The imposter syndrome of race, perpetually thrust
And imprinted unto the inflections of self

An imperialist facade.

How meaningless this all feels
What would my father say?

Late into evening
Where performance is
Finishing

He kisses my cheek and leans in, a whisper
Rich scent of bergamot
Where desire for affection continues to breed
Hopelessly futile, dissatisfied by the nature
Of companionship

It's never enough.

For him to kiss my nape, to tussle my hair,
For me to see him emerge from the waters
Of the Mexican ocean where we snorkeled
together

A lone caricature, betrothed to depression
Standing atop a tall stone crowning the palisade
Of our compound

Crying out, the patricidal
Ah!

Bemused and contained, a primordial exasperation
Refusing to be encased and becoming voluminous
Amid incandescent beams of light

Holy subterfuge diminished and obscure
Crying out once more the ceremonial
Ah!

Cathartic howls of drunken rapture
And I will offer bravery along the gates
Of Admonishment,

Coddling the affections of delimited respirations.

Site of a drunk eye flickering beneath numb mask
Of conversation, belittling and bemoaning
More kisses in the crowd between the faces of
Familiar friends gathered to say goodbye

Along the lines of the floor where the bodies meet
I can see the faces of people I once knew

Or thought for a moment I'd like to know,
And in the brief time I have been known to live

I have seen the many masks of servitude.
And I have kissed the hand of many an eager flesh

If there is a holy incumbent
They are genial at best

Lime juice seeping into open wound
Tequila– tasteless at point in evening
Misprinted memories stretching into morning
But not quite yet,

Memory interceding with recollection,
A jovial affair disquieting all fidelities of remembrance

Imagine licking the sticky floors of every dive bar you've
been to
Where you lift your shoe and you hear the interminable
CLACK!

Inflections kissing midstream, distorted chorus of flesh
Sanguine and unsound, belittling spectacle with
Unbridled jubilance,

Limbs of abstract coalescing and violently spasming
An aneurysm of beleaguered contempt
Bile spewing out in a gushing spasmodic rush
Afflicting and penetrating all withstanding benevolence

Withdrawal of affection, withering and shriveled
Drained of the artery, pulsating rhythmically
Circadian thrusts of desire being unfulfilled
Nomenclature of withholding

Anticipation forlorn and distaste commingling
Astute observation a notation in skin
Where memories are illustrated in scar tissue
A distant hissing beginning to emanate

Singularity of disposition, breathing disinterestedly
Listening with a wide aperture

To despondent claims of melancholy
Pulsing a dull throb, beats measured in minutes
Salt is wiped from the Earth in wide swaths
Sprinkled over pious wooden furrows

The Earth recoils– fetal
Weeping petulant tears aghast and afraid
Reaching up, arms outstretched, and howling
With deep and meaningless sorrow

Lascivious affection, hungering for want
To be wanted without conceding

In the streets, she's stumbling over red painted curbs
Volatile sweating profusely, speaking in singularities
In riddles pressed against each other,

Blithely firing obscenities at every hand attempting to catch her

Kissing pavement with her chin, her eyes taking separate interests
Holding blindly to curvature of the Earth,

He's following me! He's following me!
He's a fucking creep who won't leave me alone
That's what she said,

But I was there when James picked her up off the curb
With her purse spilled out   drool cradling her chin
And somehow she got into the bar I was at with a few
Other friends,

I asked him– I asked James
I thought you two left together?

And he let a sigh and wiped his brow,
No sweat or anything, just in an
Exhausted sort of way

And he says, no.

She said she was stepping out for a smoke
And she was practically falling over
So I told her I'd go up with her while she smoked outside

Then you guys were gone and she just had to come

Well thanks for looking out for her,
I'm a bit surprised they even let her in
She called me, but I told her to go home

She didn't listen

No, she didn't

I am the pause between thoughts
He said to himself

Smiling a dullard grin, beer in hand, he sang along to dull country cover band
Staring dim and jovial at daisy dukes and American
Flag bandanas being used for tops

America,
He thought to himself

What a place.

Outside there's a ripe smell of vomit and mildew,
And the wet streets of downtown San Diego are glistening
Beneath dirtied Etnies that are not up to dress code,

While sweaty men in ill-fitting dress shirts will stand outside Flux or Omnia
Waiting impatiently for a chance to go in, to dance, and to drink

To snort cocaine from the crevice of their fist in the privacy of
One-person restroom tucked behind DJ booth

Odd man out will offer to share ecstasy, but no one's
Done ecstasy since 2010, so he'll seem out of touch,
Even though it's a classy move of him to offer

People just don't know how to be gracious anymore,

Or they never did, which seems more realistic, but
Probably less palatable to those
forced to swallow it

Anyways, we're chewing ecstasy together, because
Why the hell not, I'm not there to get laid, I'm there
To dance

But that was not the group's plan, so I slipped away into the crowd
I closed my eyes, I tried just to feel, through the floor
The rhythmic pulse

I let my skin breathe
No sound but a gentle hum
Sucking all the air from the room

It was as if all sensory perception had been eclipsed
By this gentle indeterminate hum

That eagerness of sensory deprivation taking over
Immersed in the nothingness of experience

Floating where displacement occurs, and smiling
Light abruptly blinds you   and the moment
Is gone

I am everywhere   timelessness of
Recollection merges together, staggering into oblivion

Polluted by youth,
and in the excrement of candor
Self immolate

Gouge my finger nailed eyes
I am sick of looking at your staples

But the mirror rarely speaks back.

My skin looks smooth and freckled and sunspotted
And ageless all at once,

I feel veins where tears made their way
Waiting to be shot in the face where then I will
Begin to show some wear and tear

Isn't it funny how humorous it becomes.

No one ever laughs though, so I've got all
This face paint on for naught

Nothing but a naughty child being punished
For my insolence, beaten with a burlap sack
And misremembered quotes always being
Given to the wrong thought to chew on

Thought yourself a good person
Until you were reminded that you aren't.

According to whom? To you because you chose to believe it,
For what reason? Not much to it.

Reminds me of one evening when the air was humid
And it was 95 degrees at 9pm

So damp you could barely breathe without feeling
As though a damp rag had been placed over your mouth

I digress,

A return to form, to captivity, to bliss
The burning bush now a flaming tree
Golden red percolating the Earth
Where the seismic crust grips the feet
Of those it hopes to hold on to,

For the sake of memory,
Where are you?

Do you remember even when you weren't?
Can you feel it, even after all this time-
Or has time ceased to apply

And you now exist outside its bounds.

Desert Plague Doctor

The room is two-hundred dollars   a night   plus
a one-hundred dollar   non-refundable
          deposit.
So it's a pet fee?

It's   a deposit.
Yes, but it's non-refundable?
That's right.
So it's a fee.
It's   a deposit.

I waved her off and walked
Away out the lobby doors
Back to the moonlit parking lot
Where clouds commingled

With the silvery strands of light
That hung like loose threads of glimmering fabric

Angel hair caught in long eyelashes
Of evening affectations

In the car
Cat rests on center console

Briefly raises head
When I open car door

He has had a long tiresome day
On the road

Running twelve hours behind schedule
Midnight at a roadside murder of hotels
Just outside of Odessa

In the black abyssmal void
The stretch between Dallas and El Paso

Where expansion of endlessness
Finds proof of its own persistence

An ocean of black
In the dense void bloody white

Puncture wounds
Where the sinewy strands grip the Earth

In cosmic hegemony
Making eyes at the lascivious magma

Gestating below the igneous mantle
Where the lips of a flame are pursed
Pouted waiting to be yearned for

Cat gives an impatient meow
As I sit down

Places his small head
Over the crook of my folded arms

Thinking to myself   why didn't I book a hotel room
Knowing   it was because I'd planned to go further
But being   t w e l v e   hours behind it was
now late
And I was tired

Peeking out with a dim yellow glow
Just on the other side of the hotel
I could see a sign

Room $65 a night

Engine of 97' Pathfinder dutifully growled to life
Fiery pistons   restrained brakes whimpering
As foot rides pedal

Driveway lit by flickering yellow lights
Front door locked

Concierge sits smoking cigarette
at service window facing driveway

He does not acknowledge me at first,
But when I finally say hello

Slowly turns toward me with manic grin
Bulging eyes but kind delicate voice

Like echoes in ceramic cistern
Earthly disposition far beneath the radius
Of their kindly luminescence

Glow of aged electric fixtures
Blacked their silhouette

And a black beak pointed through me
Out amid the vast expanse of nothingness

Where only stars could be seen
Struggling to perambulate

Silhouette pulled back its beak
And from the gaping maw

Reeds of roses and carnations sprawled
Swept over a gushing torrential outpour

My eyes cauterized by thorny stems
Choked on the dried clippings of aged blooming tendrils

Lungs burned by
Lavender and peppermint

Gasping for a final breath
Before submersion

Sir, were you looking for a room?

You take cats?

Tum Rums

Outside there's a blanket slung over my car
Covered in vomit piss and shit
My poor cat is sitting on the kitchen table
Looking out the window with
Great big eyes both fearful and inquisitive

He turns to me then back again
To the window where outside
It has begun to rain

I can see the splash of undigested cat
Food smeared across the one side
Begin to ooze down and drip from
The tips of the comforter

Little turds on the ground
Faint smell of puke still lingering
From his small mouth

Kiss on his head,
It's not your fault, buddy.

You just got a little sick.

Trickle of a Creek

I can feel the water flowing past my feet
In the creek behind our home

It's a hundred degrees out
And the air is dense with heat

Delicate trickle of water
Flows into timid rustle of leaves

At the top of the hill that stands over the creek
I can see the greenhouse and the chicken coop

And the cottonwood pines
Just behind a small brown shape

Shifts quietly behind the golden foliage
For a moment fear

Then antlers
At the top of the hill a buck
Sunlight glowing from behind him
A yellow king surveying
his kingdom

I held my hand up,
He disappeared back over the hill.

Only a golden glow where he once stood
And the water continuing to trickle.

Abuelita

Hands are freckled and sun spotted

Memories linger
Where blemishes imbibe
Numbing agent of nostalgia

Joints of fingers
Timbre of sockets relieved of pressure
A socket for relief as well

On the counter
Bowl of freshly cut cucumbers grown in your garden
You gifted me a basket when I arrived here you know
I love mushrooms how you knew I love cucumbers too
I'll never know

Maybe it was happenstance.

I lightly salt the skinless slices the skin is a joy to crunch
But I'm not complaining and I have added a generous
amount
Of pepper and Tapatio

While I sit in the living room looking out the window at the
Glistening white landscape I can see my grandmother
eyeing
The bowl

I extend my arm bowl in hand and she looks up at me
before

Smiling the benign smile most elderly people share
Childish grin one has when you're unwilling to admit
something

She slowly reaches out and
with a delicate pluck she takes a slice of
Cucumber and puts it into her mouth

All in one fluid motion as if
the joints were made for compound movements
She an architect of motions

My grandmother is a sweet woman
She is small Mexican and native
She will not smile in photos unless you ask her to
But she is quick to laugh at nearly anything you
Present as being humorous
She laughs when she's nervous
She laughs when she's happy
She has a habit of peeing herself when she laughs too much

But nearly every member of our family farts when they
laugh or pee
There's no grace in our humor
We are all just dumb animals howling uncontrollably
Pissing wildly and shitting pants in jubilee

Would you like more cucumbers, Grandma?
Yes, Papi.

The Way Blood Coagulates

Small hoofprints in the snow
From road to my porch
Around the house

Next to the garage, beneath a tree
Circular patch of flattened snow

One large divot surrounded by
Two pale dimples punctured
by pine needles

Pieces of half-eaten watermelon
Lay on the tree stump nearby

Red drippings lead back
To the flattened snow

I can hear the dull thump
Of pine cones occasionally falling
From the yellowed trees

Snowy premature landscape
Glimmers gently
In the early blue hour

Cottonwoods hang heavy
With thick white chunks
Perched across their strained branches

Between the trees

In the snow   a red splatter

A rabbit
Who in his last moments
Looked into the abyssal eyes
huddled beneath my tree.

I shovel snow over the blood
And sit by the river,

Thinking of deer
And the way blood coagulates.

A Kiss from the River

I leaned down
And reached into the river

Felt the muddy bottom
Between my fingers

Splash of water against my lips

Seen the colorful flesh
Of a rainbow trout

Glide past my hand-

When I looked upstream
It was against the rocks of the shore

Pale belly shining,
bright and luminescent.

Deprived of Divinity

A candle on the counter smelling of vanilla macarons
Glows dimly beneath dying light of aged kitchen lightbulb

Moisture collects against windows drawing
Pools of light that form near base of the frame

A picture of the painted world
Where arms breath lavender

And cut with their stony teeth
Jeweled scepters of ash and faith

A coaxium for spasmodic blood clots
Drip like bloodied nodules of broken semi-thoughts

Line the tear ducts with firing squads
Each line a reticent melancholy platitude

Weeping outward and untoward
Ghastly display of impotence and self-immolation

In the form of emasculation
Where God weeps with disdain

That tears could flow from anything other than their
Torrential floods

Depriving their Earth of all unwanted life
Of any chance at reconciliation

Of any moment where they might turn toward
Each other and ask

What was any of it for?

Dinner with a Friend

Your fingernails are split at their ends
I can see them between your teeth

Anxious chewing, touching your face
Looking away and trying to be thoughtful
In how you answer

What would you like to eat
I'm still thinking
I don't know it all looks so good

Your shoulders lift
Trying to touch your ears

Pulling yourself inward
Making yourself small
Without realizing it

You haven't touched your water
So I tell you to drink
Finally a smile and an eye roll

You're leaning forward
While you tell me about your new job

About how it's the management role
You've wanted for some time now

Wind is pushing your golden brown hair
Into your face pell mell

But that doesn't stop you
Doesn't stifle the excitement in your voice

Occasional gasp for air
To keep going, to keep telling

With this newfound self-assurance
How you came to the director

Told them you wanted it,
And you got it.

I realized I was smiling as you told me.

Our waiter came back
You knew exactly what you wanted.

Like Charcoal Dandelions

She has eyes like the gleaming underside of leaves
With their incandescent capillaries that betray her hardness
For the tender heart that pulses beneath.

Her tiny hands with redknuckled flesh
Hard brown skin with callouses dotting
Inside of her palms.

Her thick black hair sprouts like charcoal dandelions
Where if I blow more will emerge more lustrous than
before.

Her skin iridescent and tan
Pale purple circles just beneath her eyes.

"Racoon Eyes" she calls them.

Glassy stare-
A yearning beneath long eyelashes
And thick eyebrows.

When she laughs she looks inward
As if the world isn't meant to be in on the joke.

But her sweaty palm is resting on my arm
While we sit close together
On the booth side of a restaurant table.

Said she missed me,
That she didn't need me to say it back

For her to know I felt the same way.

And I am paralyzed more than ever with
Indecision rotting my insides,

A viscous poison,
Eating away at my mangled body.

Everything hard about me has softened
And deteriorated.

I am balding and grown fat since we first met
And she has only grown more immaculate.

I wish that I deserved her.
But it doesn't stop my wanting.
Doesn't stop me when–

Outside her home, in my car,
Would you like to come in for tea?

I'd love to.

The Shape of Light Passing Through Water

I feel the damp sleet   crunching beneath my feet
Tiny specks of moisture float down on to my cheeks
My nose red with cold   eyes watering at slight breeze

Air smells new
The Earth's dirt has been turned
Its naked ground now exposed
Breathing for the first time anew

Sky is a black tapestry bespeckled
With beauteous dim puncture marks
Flesh wounds of the cosmic fangs
Piercing in perpetuity

Tightly holding hands with oblivion
A kiss for the spectral portions
Of the universe.

No butterflies around
Only black bears that emerge from
Thick snowy foliage

Occasional trout swimming downstream
A rooster crows and its bright squawk
Illuminates the valley below

Light cascades over cracked and gutted
Landscape   plateau overlooking valley

Where clouds hang low and dark
Heavy with tempestuous rage

Unwieldy stratocumulus bold and benign
Pregnant with density of moisture
Tension of electricity

I am struck by the shape of light that passes through water
From beneath its surface I claw at the icy barrier to air
From the cracked visage distorted with impurities
I weep without teardrops

There is only air in the water
And I am gasping for every particle.

You're a Goose

There's bare walls all white and dusty like an unused journal
That you maybe only ever wrote a few lines in
Where you tried to find your voice or at least
The rhythm you'd expose yourself to folding
Inward like the abstract coils shapelessly shifting
Inordinate and indifferent

And things just sort of happen

In this hotel room where outside the thick windows
Construct starts and stops in fits and the sound of
Metal scraping against metal and a musical ringing
From their friction echos out between the towering
Masses of concrete and steel

Shapes having been forgotten
And at the bedside a paper cup filled to the brim with champagne
Thin white sheets that aren't
Warm enough when the A/C runs and cold enough when it doesn't

Thinking of old hands
Way the skin is all thin and veiny
And delicate and
There's a softness to the way
They grab you
And hold you so firm all at once

Tenacity of misery is a persistent bugger

That has been thoroughly kissed and flicked
Between the eyes irritatingly during all times
Of the days and the afternoons which for some
The day only begins after the sun has peaked
But for others the days start and end in darkness

A goose will ask for a kiss and honk

As if we all aren't honking along idiotically because what else is there to do
But to honk loudly and annoyingly hoping for the love of God that across the
Room we will be noticed for our feathers and remembered for their bright
Vibrant colors

Only you're a Goose, not a peacock.
Hell- you're not even a duck.

Sunlight Paints the Concrete Canvas

Flavorless-
My jaw is sore and the fellow at the car wash is struggling
To find something trapped beneath his passenger seat

Meanwhile
There's a construction crew guiding cars down a narrow
Pathway that's only wide enough for one flow at a time

Traffic
Is backed up but there's no honking, everyone has just
Sort of accepted their fate and resigned themselves

And sweat,
Because in this heat there's no relief
In anything but maybe a plate of fresh garlic fries

Outside the Mexican cafe
People are sitting at small two-person tables
Drinking glasses of Clamato and Modelo

Steam rises from the
Kitchen window out the side of the cafe building
Where a dishwasher sits on a short wall smoking a cigarette

Apron
Slung over his shoulder,
Sweat gathered at the nape of his t-shirt
Server standing across from him, arms folded and stern-

faced

Air is heavy
With humidity and sunlight paints the concrete canvas
Thick round glasses rimmed with Tajin and a fresh cut lime slice

Micheladas and chilaquiles
Are the only things I want in this moment, but I'm
Bereft of cash at a cash-only establishment

Inside there's an ATM
That keeps spitting my card out, but the woman
At the counter tells me to bring the cash next time and takes my order anyways

Warm
Plate set down at my little table, smell of salsa and fried eggs
Black beans and potatoes, glass filled to the brim a bright luminous red

Thank you, I say to the man who sets my plate down.
De nada, he says in return.

I use one of my napkins
To wipe the sweat from my forehead
Grab my fork and dig in

Across the street
I can see a new taco spot has opened up recently
With glistening white tiles and an ornate flower mural

It advertises five-dollar tacos and will close in several

months
When the residents refuse to abandon their local taquerias

A man pushing his paletas cart down the hot sidewalk stops
Just a few feet away from my table,

¿Quieres una paleta, joven?
No cash, I'm sorry.
Andale pues, he nods and keeps rolling.

I eat before my food becomes soggy.

Tropic of Asphalt

There are enough books to fill
Four parking spaces

Folding tables are arranged in rows
Beneath a thin canvas canopy

His van is parked against the lot
And he sits in the open side door smoking cigarettes

Only about half the books are out of the van on the tables
And a young boy is meticulously perusing each box

Beyond the lot of books there are throngs of vendors
Sprawled across the parking lot

Each offering their own selection of goods:

Books - Clothes - Tools - Antiques - Toys
Fruit - Flowers - Donuts - Pet Care - Electronics
Phone Repair - Shoe Shine - Massage - Video Games
Weapons - Car Floor Mats - Rugs - Guayaberas

There is the occasional couple or family who have come
To sell the extra things they've had sitting in their home
For years and they thought they'd make some money

It's usually a couple with only one parking spot
And their 20-year old Honda Civic

With a single blanket laid out on the pavement

And a pile of clothes, maybe some baby toys,
Other benign belongings that don't sell

And they've spent fifty dollars to sit in the heat
With no covering to make maybe a hundred bucks
In the whole afternoon

This is not the place for those folks,
And yet there's always at least one
Who has yet to learn their lesson

After picking several books he thinks might be interesting
Boy holds a pile up for the bookseller to see.

Ten for the four of them, seems right.
I'd do eight.

The man smiles to himself, pulling another cigarette
From the torn pocket of his oil-stained t-shirt

You can look through anything in the van you want
Long as you unload them when you do.

Boy thinks about it, hand to his chin staring at the ground
Eyebrows scrunched together looking older than he is

Find enough and we'll talk price again.

In the back of the van the boxes are arranged like
An overcrowded bookstore

And the floor is a narrow channel
The small boy must navigate

He looks through a box then carries it
Out of the van and drop its onto a table

He repeats this process until the back of
His shirt is drenched   beads of sweat
Roll down his temples

He stands with his
Hands on the back of his hips, looking up
At the sky from the back of the half-empty van
Where the canopy doesn't cover

He sees the white clouds hanging
Like splashes underwater reflecting
The currents of the ocean

Serenity of sunlight and sweat and quietness–somehow.

Boy smiles to himself,
ready to negotiate once more.

A Blur in Light

every morning

Just outside my window
Tiny body wings flapping
So quickly they're a blur in light
Suspending their small form.

In the early golden light their feathers
Glow like old depression era glass
And their needle-thin beak buries itself
In floral uterus.

I try to hear the hum.

Moments– a car starts down the road
then a silhouette against the pale sky.

Five Degrees is Bearable

I'm smoking a cigarette in the laundry room
negative 16 degrees outside
Cold   hurts to breathe.

Five degrees is bearable,
But negative   is where I draw the line.

Can't do it.

Little stabs in your chest   body fights to acclimate.
Hands are ill-prepared.

My brother steps outside,
It's not so bad.

Give it three minutes, I tell him.

He laughs   three minutes
He's back inside rubbing his hands together
Breathing into his palms
Speaking as if he has run out of breath.

Boy, that really knocks the wind out of you, don't it?

I laughed.

You should have smoked in the bathroom near the fan.
Yeah, you're probably right.

I dropped my cigarette into a mostly empty soda can

And shrugged my shoulders.

Next time.

My Sleepy Cat

My cat is sleeping on the back of the couch–

He is resting behind my head
His little back paw is nuzzling my shoulder

Every once in a while he stretches
And the soft pads of his feets touch my cheek
Or his tail wraps itself around my neck
under my chin

I bury my face in the fur of his tummy
Kissing him and reminding him what a brave prince he is
For traveling all this way

Do I wish he were a smidgen more
Accommodating with his kennel?

Perhaps, but he's very good about
Sitting on my lap in the car and sleeping
While I drive along the highway

Or riding the center console
Watching the scenery pass us by

His eyes are glossy
Black holes set in precious green stone
Balsamic resting in a pool of olive oil

His paw grips his gut
Pulling itself closer to his white whiskers

With his broad dramatic licks

His gray and black coat
Shedding away in the summers
But thick and industrious for these harsh winters

I caught the little bastard
Drinking out of the toilet the other day
One foot in the bowl for leverage

Horrifying.

He will only drink running water, and you must be there to
Guard him
While he drinks, otherwise it's not safe, so he'll just wait
Until you're ready.

Unless of course it's a toilet bowl,
But he and I talked about that,
And he's gonna do better.

I'm not sure I believe him.

The Antlered Crown

We'd worried about driving in the dark

Up the mountain
moribund sunlight gave a final exasperated sigh

In the darkness of the mountain road
Slowly up the pass where tall cottonwood trees
Loomed

Brief glimpses in the darkness
Of even darker silhouettes
And the occasional glow of eyes

Just as we'd thought to laugh
Out into the road a white-tail

Gentle slowdown,
Out of the headlights
Into the darkness

Further on   even slower pace
Nervous laughter

Eyes darting   between
Rearview   and road

Wasn't long before we
Crossed paths again,

An unwieldy shadow

Emerged with great antlered crown
Immense royalty of the woods

Vast and mammoth
At first we saw just the one
Near edge of the road

A colossal throng of keratin branches
Stretched out from its monumental skull

I looked to my right into the darkness
Three large shapes stood even taller
Even more ghastly in size
All-consuming of what little light remained

Spectral steeds of gargantuan stature
Stared at us with unblinking eyes
Black and immutable in the black
Of the mountainous abyss

I kissed the black screen of night
With tender fearful eyes
And let my gasps breath light
Into the small aperture
Of the starry spectral evening

My lymphs dotted the canvas
with glittering puncture wounds
Where the silvery flesh could
Peacefully drip for eternity

Void filled rapidly with endlessness
Expanding breathlessly

My breaths expanding to its container
Lungs exploding in mess
Of guttural fluids

Silvery beads of fluid
Dripped from the end
Of the celestial rod

A broad stroke of light
Smeared across the black
Veneer of time in memoriam

Let ring heavenly tantalizing sirens
Soundless and penetrating
Peerless and perpetual

In those black roadside apparitions
Where bone bathed in velvet

Dressed the thorny crown
That drew nothingness from oblivion

Its lines etched into ether
Eternity smiles blissfully.

Drive… I finally said.
And over the mountain we flew in the night.

Watching Deer Eat

I'm lying in bed trying to jack off
But I can't think of much

So I'm working with something
That's only half-stiff

Eventually I capitulate

Pour myself a cup of coffee
And look in the fridge

Hoping for something new to materialize
But each time I am disappointed

My boredom is hungry

I sit on the porch smoking cigarettes
Watching the deer eat the rind of watermelon
and apple cores I set out for them

Still for a moment
Watching with beady black eyes
Ears taut and upward

Their mouths caked in red
A bloodied palette.

A clump of snow falls from branch nearby
They flit into the cover of dense forest.

Little Intimacies

There is no face I would rather look at
Than yours

More than all the paintings of the Earth
I would rather admire the small lines that
Form the edges of your eyes
Your strands of silvery gray hair
That fall across your hooked nose
Which you affectionately refer to as your schnozz.

I would rather switch plates with you because
You liked what I ordered better
More than the cooked salmon which you always
Get because you want to be healthy and
Because you always feel like maybe you just
Haven't given it a fair shake or gone to the right
Spot,

it must be hard to cook that's got to be it
But you let me have your baked potato because
You know I love a baked potato and I eat it whole
Which always makes you laugh but you like that about me

Or at least you make me feel like you do and
You give me little kisses on my ears from
Behind with your arms wrapped around my neck

You are always wanting to hug and
Rarely wanting to be hugged
So when I come home and there you

Are on the couch with your arms out
I hold on extra tight and I'm last to let go
Because I like you to know that

I don't want to let go.

I Drank Too Much Too Early

Trying to keep your eyes open in the midday sun,
bright reflection of light from the sea of glimmering white snow,

Is nearly impossible.

I'm wearing spanish style wraparound sunglasses in the town store
Our grand town of eight-hundred people.

My parka is too large for the narrow aisles
My hood keeps catching on the clips
they hang bags of chips from.

I reflexively turn around
Yanking string of plastic'd treats to the ground

Loud crackle of air-filled bags
Wracking up against one another,

I've poked my head up from between the aisles and made eye contact
With the cashier, who has managed to tug herself from indifference
Briefly enough to glance up at me.

I *feel* suspect.

Like walking out of a store without purchasing anything
You feel like you've broken the law.

I am *technically* breaking the law,
But that's neither here nor there.

She returns to her task,
Counting money at the register.

It's been some time for me,
Since I've done that sort of work I mean.

I had a whole gambit of jobs before I landed here.

The warehouse jobs
were fun   but they paid poor

And the restaurant jobs
were hard   but decent tips

And the customer services jobs
were both unfun   and poorly paid

I'll never *not* tip again in my life.
A waiter would have to call my mother a trollop
To her face at the table for me not to tip.

And even then I'd probably still tip ten percent.

The only customer worse than a hungry customer
Is a customer who needs to be right.

I would see people return drills that had very clearly been used,
Little bits of cement and sawdust stuck to their plastic shells

And they'd try to return it with a receipt from 2007…
from a different store.

And you wouldn't believe the commotion they'd cause.

I'd like to speak to your manager.
I'd like for you to fuck off.

It's my **right** as a customer.
It's your right to fuck all the way off.

I can assure you I'll never shop here again.
I can assure you, I still don't give a fuck.

I will not act grateful for the chance to make starvation wages.
Take it back I will *act*, but I will not *be*.

There is no thanks to be given when they've stolen what little dignity
You gave up on taking this job.

But I've thought too long about this.

And the cashier is furrowing her brow concerningly,
Did I say any of that out loud?

I hold my hand out expecting change,
but her demeanor changes to questioning,

So I pull my hand back, an infantile fist against my chest,
and purse my lips, unsure.

A pause as I look at her, to the floor, then back again to her.

Commitment is the best route in these situations,
So I begin to pick from the counter–

-one carton Camel filters
-two cans ice mocha coffees
-several boxes of sleep aid ear plugs
-a bag of spicy chicharrónes
-and a gallon of antifreeze

Would you like a bag? She asked. Every question a question mark.

No, no, this is fine, I say raising my hand then plucking up the antifreeze.

And after a momentary lapse in thought it occurs to me at some point
I took my sunglasses off.

Again, I am caught in an extended pause.
I smile and look around, trying to find purpose,

But there is none.

I walk towards the door, facing the cashier, nudging it open with my butt
As I slip out back into the blinding midday light.

God, I'm tired.

The Dried Wrinkles of the Earth

From atop the precipice of a vast expanse
Land is carved with etchings of memory
Imprints and scars commiserating
Indifferently,

Smeared makeup of a callous face
Kissing moonlight
As fogs hug the dim evening asphalt
In the early morning hours

A veneer of twinkling dew
Sheath for the stained dagger
Dripping with starry discharge
And silvery ichor,

Pulled from the fleshly pocket
It created
Wounding further with its absence
Metallic coagulation being broken
And resealed and broken again

An aging face
Being drawn upon
A life illustrated

Fingers run across the valleys
And divots and junctures
Where time found itself

Punctured by the crossings

Of paths that could be
And often never were

Where time sits and thumbs
Through leaflets describing
The long passage
That stretches on endlessly

Each page unevenly cut
And scrawled across its rough
Surface are aphorisms soaked
In pungent red wine

Fingers run across the pages
Bringing back memories of touch
Of fingertips gently colliding
Then sustaining

Memories of thoughts that never came to be
Only wishful thinking in the late evenings
While drenched and soaked in melancholy

Grappling with the space memory once occupied
Holding dearly to the hand outstretched
So close desire and sensation are conjoined

That the thought remains a memory
So close the memory germinates
It becomes an imprint carved in flesh

Heart collapses and folds inward
Fingers dig into the Earth

Flakes of dirt crumble from between
Crevices of fingers crushing Earthly matter
Stained with the moonlit tears
And ephemeral bliss of catharsis

From between the pieces of crushed Earth
That scatter in the delicate evening breeze
Pieces of a purple hyacinth perforate the
Black sod beneath knees

Hands scoop the Earth in great momentous mounds
And from within its tranches a face emerges

Pale and flawless smooth as the moon
On a cloudless evening sky

It begins to dry and wither and crumple until
Only the petals of a dead flower remain

And in the dried riverbeds where water that flowed
Once reflected the beautiful irises of Narcissus

A sparse bed of pale flowers remains.

I lie down in the bed and begin to weep,
For I never had the chance to gaze upon those eyes.

Breaths Between Eternities

I'm hunched in the creek
behind our house,

Neighbors had taken rocks
And damned up part of the creek

So the water pools into one area
Funneled into a narrow channel before moving downstream

In the center of the pool
is a small pile of rocks stacked atop each other

I don't much believe in superstition,
But I recall hearing somewhere it's bad luck to tip them
over

So I decide against it despite my natural inclinations.

In thirty-five degree weather,
I feel the heat rapidly dissipating from my legs

There's a river trout wading just near the glassy surface,
He's only a few feet away

Distant odor of firewood burning,
It suddenly occurs to me that the fire ban in Wyoming
Probably only applies to outdoor fires

I feel duped.

I'm inching closer to the trout,
His head is turned so a single eye faces me from the side
Of its glistening head, indirect light reflecting across its skin

There is a moment-

A stillness between us

Nature has paused to spectate,
There is only silence and the delicate sound of water streaming
Out of the pool and further down the creek

A tender breeze pushes clumps of snow from the branches of an overarching
Tree and they break the glassy surface of the creek with several splashes.

Trout retreats behind the cairn as I stab my hand into the water,
I miss and my balance is shaken,

Instinctively,
I attempt to grab hold of the stone pillar
And its many stones tumble over with me into the water

I am submerged in darkness for years.

Where I will plant my roots and breathe through the Earth
My tendrils eloquently sprawling across the pool's floor,

Beneath the ground and up the subsurface cavern walls
Until my heart beats in synchronicity with the pulsing
Core of our universe's center,

Breaths between eternities,
And a rhythmic arterial thump
Almost imperceptible,

The sloshing of dogma
Folding over itself habitually without end
Gesticulating adoringly,

An orchestra of conception

The molten precipice being birthed and rebirthed before me,
Pieces being stitched together in beauteous unison.

And I have ceased to exist as anything other than everything,

The rusting of tree leaves, the pale water flowing down the narrow creek channel
An amoeba of consciousness that has dispersed across all of the observable
And inobservable world

Bound by nature to exude solemnity and indifference,
But looking on with deep love and affectation

I am in a scalding hot shower inside my home,
Trying to burn away the memories of despair

Thinking of how I could once effortlessly catch fish.

All That Is Beautiful Trying To Kill You

When I went to sleep last night there were small jewels floating through the air like tiny gems reflecting in the moonlight,
Melting into the grass as they landed, you can always smell the change of moisture in the air
Itself a good omen of sorts,
A sign of inevitability accompanied by the overstrong breeze turned gusts that will gently carry your spirits to the single digits,
Where in the early morning you rise and it is still dark,

But as the lone streetlamp shines between the cracks of the kitchen blinds, a streetlamp you yourself pay two dollars a month for because the city doesn't do that this far outside its bounds

You will see a pearlescent white field shining back at you

Its gilded white surface glistening and immaculate, kissing the earth with a cold patience
Opening the front door to the chilling air, cold enough to
Sting your lungs and strain your bronchioles with swelling and affectation

Overwhelmed with sentiment
And at first it's not so bad in those initial seconds
In the intervening moments you can feel the heat
Begin to leave your body

Warm fickle tears carving their path down your face
As you delicately weep

Your tears so small and understated,
Like the motions of a body inertia unable to stop
The path before carved and carved again
Worn down enough to be desired

Trying to understand why
How these years later you can still smell sage
And have to grip a nearby rail

Stunned with paralysis as the song comes on
Trying to park, but you've got to pull over

You can't breath
The air is being wrought from your frail
Figure until only bodily dust remains
Pulverized and beaten and crushed

All to yourself.

You've always had me to yourself,
Only you never really knew it
Or you knew it and chose not to
Or maybe we just like the inbetween

Maybe we're meant to be what-ifs
Maybe we're growing old together just thinking about it

Maybe that's enough,
I don't think it is, but it's better than nothing

I'm looking back at the front door and at the side of the house I can see a thin trail of cloven hooves that pass from along the side to the back near the stream where the snowy bluff overlooks the mountain pass

I'm following the path and beneath the bushes near the back window there's an imprint in the snow where they like to sleep, huddled close together

Sometimes in the evening while I sit at the kitchen table quietly eating alone I'll see the light of the front lamp, its path interrupted for a brief moment from between the blinds

And there is a shape that's almost imperceptible by the space it occupies, brown button nose betrays it among the lighter browns of its fur and the trees and the glimmering white snow

A mask for affection to be worn by those that are brave enough to wear.

I haven't heard a human voice in days. How long can it be? There is pale dust up to the top of my porch now, and I can't open my screen door without pushing against a mound of powder

And wiping my feet before coming inside is hell because there's always snow that gets in and melts and wets the carpet, and it's not like I can open the doors to air it out

The walls are no longer warm enough

I can feel my skin peeling away at the inlay
Where the stitching meets the muscle
Timbre of my shape being hollowed out
And burned away

excrement of a fleshly sculpture
sculptor with her pick chipping away at remnants
Trying to expose the shape amid the arterial stone

Every jab of her rasp-

A gouge to my insides, wearing my innards obliquely
Even little nodes being shapen into strands of hair
Where soft veiny marble was once smooth and submissive
Awaiting its shaping, my teetering body trembling with fear
And agony

Every singular cell of my body as in unison to the detriment of agony
To the orchestration of displeasure and self exposition

I am exposed, utterly exposed
Naked to all, but myself

So I will claw away at the insides of this sarcophagus
Until my nails are broken and splintered at my fingertips

And when my hair begins to fall in great tufts of bushy black
Brillow pads being blown astray and tumbleweeded along

My eyes will be red circles drained of every last memory,
Of every ache I have to give

And I will fall to my knees in the snow,
These the shortest two minutes of my life

The feeling from my legs gone
So cold at once, now so hot

My shirt is falling away in pieces and the sun is burning away the low
Hanging fog where its waves of light begin to crest just over the top of that hill

I'm reaching up towards it on all fours with tears
Returning to my eyes utterly blinded by the golden reciprocity of the snow

It has been so long and all at once
I feel compounded by time, a threshling ashore and incapable

What was it all for?

As if every moment only mattered in that moment
And every moment thereafter in itself self concerned
Or more perhaps indifference

Youthful depravity has left me and in its place is the battered near middle age misanthrope who is aging tastelessly and disarmingly

All that was once beautiful has worn away to memories of something more beautiful
than ever was

It was only a few days ago as I was washing dishes I could see a silver f-150 pull into our snowpacked driveway, large tires with well worn ridges

Stopped a few feet from the front porch and out came this small man who'd been by a few days earlier to look at my garage door when it got stuck

In his hands I could see he was carrying a small package as he knocked on the door,
Hold on! Let me get my mask

He smiled and nodded at me through the window when I held my arm up to say so
I dug through the pile of clean but unfolded clothes resting in the living room recliner

I pulled the straps of the mask over my ears and opened the door

Hey there, how are ya today?
I'm good, good. Just lying around enjoying the morning, drinking too much coffee I think.

Oh, that sounds great. I'm fighting a hangover myself.
No such thing as too much whiskey in this weather.
You're right about that. Wanted to stop by, wasn't sure if you like eggs...

I love eggs.

...I've got eggs from my chicken here and I wanted to bring

you some.
Yes, wow, that's amazing, thank you. I appreciate it.

It's nothing, don't think anything of it. My wife Judith is in the car there,
He pointed to the truck where a hand could be seen waving from behind the fogged windshield.

I thanked him.
He got back into his truck and drove away.

I drove along the highway later that afternoon and as I looked out all that could be seen was a vast pale landscape, punctured by ruptures of the Earth, themselves overflowing with soft wintery powder

Every sight feels so definitive, so absolute.

On the left mountains rose high above the road even higher so above the expansive plains stretched far beneath and before them

A blanket for the Earth to be worn and warmed.

On the road there is a snowy aurora dancing beautifully across the white speckled asphalt
My golden Saturn glides effortlessly through this bleak and gorgeous landscape, leaves white ripples coursing through the frigid air

When it is this cold the engine turns very slowly and the windows will sometimes refuse to open and the gear shifter will stick until it has thawed with the engine running

And in some cases the spring in your garage door opener will unwind, giving slack in the cables that hoist the door causing them to tangle.

So then it's six at evening in 15 degree snowfall, you're attempting to shut your garage bay door

But it's no use.

The tip of your nose will begin to burn, as will your cheeks, and your fingertips. Blood rushing to them, attempting to compensate and combat.

I'm drinking a hot toddy right now and thinking of the cold heightens the experience.

The night cloaks the earth, a small circle of light from our streetlamp holding the darkness back from total enshroudment.

The wind blows the ice parallel to the ground, a sharp mist stinging my face and my hand as I try to smoke a cigarette.

Negative degree weather is uninviting (to the antiquated smokers).

Coffee not enough   whiskey not enough
My hands are   jointsweldedtogether
A   singular   mass
Incapable of m o v e m e n t
Struggling to shift my orbital axis

Betrothed to immobility.

From the edges of darkness I see a small shape begin to emerge,
Brown button nose betraying figure once more

Usually so alert, but now trusting
Inching close, sniffing the ground
Not making eye contact, not yet

I shuffle my boots against the snow encrusted porch,
Ice scraping against my heel

But nothing. No acknowledgement.
Still no eye contact

There was a bear spotted in town recently and now every time I go out to smoke at night, I am watchful of the corners of the house on each side of me

I want to cover my face with my parka hood to shield me from the wet stings of the snow being blown into my face, but it's not worth the risk of diminished peripherals

It's in the silence of these moments-

Where the only sound you can hear is the Earth breathing between leaves
An indifferent language to its exhalations-

That I think *to what purpose* any of it has

I think of how ambitious I once was

Or how hopeful and spritely

And how nostalgia scrubs the memory
of all that is unbecoming

I will awkwardly say hello one day
And spend the rest of my life wondering if I should have raised my hand
To say hello or lowed the timbre of my voice to be more warm
More welcoming, less aloof, more present

In the morning when I am cooking the eggs my neighbor brought me I will
Cherish the richness of their yolk, the full bodied whites that simmer and bubble
And taste a great canvas of flavor wrought from the love and affection
He pays those chickens each day when he takes the time

To care for them.

They are fed and warm as I am fed and warm
I am nourished by the kindness of others
And perplexed by the emptiness of ulterior motives
How for no other reason than to give,

They give.

How in the morning when I rise to feed my cat and give him water from the faucet
As he refuses to drink sitting water,

I will hear a rooster echo from the mountain breathing its own indifferent breath into
The earth that has fed it

The creek behind our home will continue on as it always has,
Whispering with cool temperament things only it can perceive

And the sun will peak up from behind its foggy curtain to illuminate the hillside
And give the overnight fluff its golden hue

How immaculate to feel the soft crunch of snow before it has compressed and bonded
With its many layers, a divine secret of conception

At the stream's edge, there, a lone fish treads, leaving momentary ripples of the surface
That eventually coagulate with the stream's glossy mirror

Removing my glove, I kneel down and gently slide my hand beneath the surface,
And immediately its warm is propagated back whence it was birthed,

Into the mantle shaped by magma I am reaching, deeper, wholly enveloped
What remains lies charred and ashed,

And rebirthed the Earth gravitates towards life,
Illuminating the tundra of despondency

Refusing to look away it will burnish the rapturous discord
And wail unceasingly,

A cosmonic siren-

HOWLING LISTLESSLY! Great modes of destruction being carved into
The very tablets of being, where they will be mounted atop the hill
As holy gravemarkers for the interpretation of time as it once was
How time ceased to be when it ceased to be interpreted

There is nothing still and entirely frozen all at once.

Lying, as one does, to oneself and upon the snowy ground.
All that is beautiful trying to kill you.

Where You Once Sat

You were on the floor trying to pet my cat,
But he remains offput by your energy

Comin' in too hot, I told her.
He'll come around.

She had a gift for me.
From her purse she pulled a small box
And said it was nothing,

I cut the bow on the box with my little knife
And pulled the top off,

Inside was a small cat leash.

I know you probably can't use it,
But I saw it in Mexico and I had to get it for you.

She once gave me a pilea, my first plant,
And even though I didn't know how to care for it
I kept it on the cusp of life for years

When we enter the restaurant there is a middle-aged
Mexican woman
Who asks us in Spanish how many are eating

I hold up my fingers and say–   three
The waitress points us to a table in the back and disappears
into the kitchen

I want a bloody more than anything right now.
I don't think they do bloody's here.
Really? Is it like beer only? They do margaritas, it says…

When the waitress comes to take our order,
She tries to order a bloody, but settles for a margarita

I order a michelada. We cheers.

La cuenta, por favor!

I've got this one.
No, you can't, that's too much.
You're always treating, let me buy my friend dinner for once.
Alright, fine, but I'm paying for your drinks at the bar.
That's fine.
What kind of place is it?
It's a dingy little dive bar. Locals know it.
Oh, that sounds fantastic.
It's maybe not even a dive bar, more just like a dirty hometown bar if that makes sense, like I always end up running into someone from high school there every time I come back.
Yup yup, I get exactly what you're saying.

We walk at a leisurely pace down third avenue
In downtown Chula Vista
All the outdoor patios that had replaced parking stalls
Overstuffed with people

You can hear music blasting from every brewery
Every restaurant we pass
Smell of tacos, quesadillas, mariscos, birria, and adobada

All commingle with the ocean air
Wafting in from the nearby harbor

Light glows in alleys between buildings lining the avenue
You can see down F street past the police station
The public library–the sun falling below palm trees
That line the parking lot of City Hall

Top of the parking structure
We smoke a cigarette and you laugh
Because you'd only tried smoking once
And we both know you'll have a cigarette
Hangover tomorrow

Inside the bar
It's filled with aging locals
Some swollen with years of hard drink
Others youthful just beginning their lives
And more even middle-aged mexican couples
Wearing Chargers jerseys, sporting white high socks
And bearing a number of tattoos

What they all have in common is a love of bad dancing
And even worse karaoke

You kneel down to pet a dog
I can't remember the dog's name,
But the man who's with her is nice

We sit together,
You have your one drink
While I slam tequilas

Down my gullet

You take my phone and as we scroll through the photos
There on the screen–the three of us

Finally you stop and look at me for what feels like a long time
I look back at you and neither of us says anything until finally
You look away

What are you thinking–I can never read you

Your eyes hung on me a long time
And I didn't say anything
I just smiled and finished my drink

C'mon, it's time to go

You sit with me at the bus stop
While I smoke a cigarette
And we wait for our cab to get here

In the intervening moments
I can feel the dense humid night
And the squalor of human sadness

Singular glow of my cigarette
You sitting next to me
Looking down at your feet

We're quiet together
And the street is empty

Marine layer had begun to settle in

Our cab pulls up.

And we both get in,
empty seat between us.

Cruelty Hiding In The Throes Of Envy

Cat   perched on bookshelf,
Looking over   living room
Regal– aloof   side-eyeing

A handless ring,
Resting in perpetuity

I sneak out to smoke,
I'm supposed to be quitting but
One in the evening never hurt
Or anyway it's fine

to breathe
An immeasurable gasp of
Sulfite and masochism

tears in
Overflowing shot glass
Wet imprint of ring

took shelter
Under eaves of depression
Eased into melancholy and
Habitual self abuse

Starvation in the arms of sagging
Skin   at a loss for flesh
And spine

feeling stretched thin
Seething a calcite grimace
Quiet and taciturn

Lit by all means a candle wick
Extinguished by ending of its
Waxing arrhythmia

Procession of condolences
Cortege-lined streets   haven
To faded inklings of alleged genius
Of alleged kindness

A benevolent subterfuge

Of cruelty hiding in the throes of envy
Dispiriting lust never quite fulfilled in the
Ether of despondency

Sound of rain outside now impatient
Telegraph that it is

Decoding its messages are ringlets–
Pallbearers in wight gowns
A floral casket being perched and held afloat
By a flock of mourning ravens

There's no pain or indifference only
Nothingness,

Perpetually punctuated by ill
Fatigued rappings–

Feverous – a cavernous howl
Portends the illusive sight of closure

A cloister of flesh embolizing
Collapsing sinews, their buttresses falling
            the ageless cathedral

In recompense
A seizure of indentured body

Every one of them betrothed to grief
Every one of them betrothed to misery
Consummating their grief and misery
In orgies of despair

We are standing in the aisle together, I'm walking down in my suit
I'm holding back tears, It's unbecoming

But in the delicate gaze of immortals there is a spritely laugh
I imagine it must echo like light peaks its eye above mountaintops

An excerpt of existence being illustrated right before my eyes
Strokes of dawn tenderly taking your hand

Guiding the ferry from aisle to isle.

Little Gems

We had spent the night drinking together in a bar.

I was surprised, when she initially asked me out
I was a few drinks in and feeling bold...

She smiled at me from behind her glass of rose'
as she took careful, deliberate sips

Waiter brought new drinks
and explained how the restaurant worked

It was to be a four-course dinner with no substitutions
except in cases of allergies

Of which neither of us had any.

It also came with a pairing of wine to match each course
beautifully presented by a handsome staff with fantastic
teeth

First Course: ***Little Gems***
hard boiled duck egg
red onion
parsley
dried cranberries
danish blue (not entirely sure what that is)
bacon vinaigrette

Eggs are one of my favorite foods
perhaps only competing with rice and shrimps

Two runny eggs between slices
of slightly toasted white bread slathered
with a thick layer of mayo

Single slice of sharp cheddar cheese
it makes me exceptionally happy

She on the other hand
abhors her eggs even the slightest bit runny
they came sunny side up

She carved out the egg whites
and I removed the yolk to my plate

I don't particularly recall the wine
never been much of a connoisseur but
my mother conflates how often I drink it
with the amount of expertise I must have

She finds me to be quite informed.

Second Course ***Wood Grilled Scallops***
            coal roasted corn
            mango salsa
            fermented mushroom butter
            puffed rice

I love mushrooms
not as much as eggs

but you hand me a bowl of mushrooms
and I will eat it

When I was a child
my godmother learned this about me

and every day, no matter the meal
my dish came with a side of sauteed mushrooms

piled above the rim of the bowl

She used to run through pounds and pounds
of mushrooms for me each month and somehow
I never grew tired of them

I must have been about 15.

The bit I'm less fond of is the mango salsa
Sweetness doesn't go there

We kept talking, kept laughing
it felt very natural

She had been to my home before
with her boyfriend

There was one night in particular where
she and I were both absolutely sloshed
and we got to talking music

It wasn't long before I'd thrown a record on and
we were shouting out lyrics to music from our youths

Our neighbors were bartenders so they were
never home to hear the raucous next door

Except once coming home after a night out
roommates were in the street

His girlfriend– red-faced and screaming.

He's at least five inches taller than her
but she towered over him– dense with rage

He was trying to make himself as agreeable as possible
but she was having none of it

She kept screaming
our neighbors in a rare display came
out from their house and started yelling as well

We're calling the fucking cops if you don't get her inside.

Third Course ***Hamachi Tartare***
black sesame
cilantro
avocado
sprouts
cucumber
trout roe
taro root chips

The roe is very important to me not on its own
but as an accent it really ties the dish together

On their own they're just salty little fish eggs that
have been cured but they give the dish that last little flair

They're the red streak in the sky
the afterglow of a profound sunset

On their own merely enjoyable
but when paired as such simply immaculate

This is all very extra of me I understand that
but what's the point of life if not to go the extra mile

I remember the days when the three dollar
bottle of champagne was a treat

While I savor those moments and treasure
what they meant– why would you ever go back?

We had to make our own
pleasures– find them where we could

Because the world is a hungry beast
constantly hungering for the misery of others

As quickly as it will grant you profound epiphany
atop mountain bluff overlooking a lake with tears
of joy chiseling their path down your face

you will just
as quickly make a single misstep and fall
to your very certain doom

Or worse you'll lose your feet to frostbite
and win an award presented by a shoe store

Life seems to thrive on the misery of others.

And yet
we dig out every last morsel of pleasure we can
I spend so much time thinking– what the point of any of it
is

There's no great answer– there's no overarching plot.

You just come home every day after a long time at work
and you struggle to pick something to eat and if you're
anything like me it's usually Mexican

When I moved away to Texas I couldn't stand the
Mexican food so I learned how to make a lot of my favorite
dishes myself

Life is funny like that.

And eventually everything you've done or everyone you
knew is forgotten
not even forgotten but erased in the immeasurable passage
of time

Eventually we all cease to exist and the idea
that we ever did is lost with us– lost with those
who still remembered

And long after humanity has failed and Earth's
core has imploded the universe will still be here
existing as it always has because
even in its vast emptiness it existed

The idea of

nothing is in turn something.

You can only theorize its improbability
And even that is a stretch in the cosmonic scheme of things

I forget what the fourth course was.

Twin Suns

I keep having dreams of you
This morning I woke up freezing
You'd left the air conditioner on

So I got out of bed and
Dragged my underweared behind
To the kitchen to make some coffee
And feed our cat (you like to say he's *my* cat)

Clock on the oven glowed 4.08am

I saw myself in the mirror
Turned to the side and looked
At my gestating tummy beginning
Its conquest of my waistline

My growing breasts
And their plump nipples
Tiny black dots bordering
Areolas where I had shaved
Long black strands

My thin ruffled hair
I could see the light through
And the exposed scalp that used
To hide under much thicker tresses

You were still in bed
Breathing slow–deep

And for a few moments
Your breaths reminded me
Of how you used to get panic attacks
When we first started dating

Or you'd have little fits in your sleep
So I'd hold you until you were still again

You sleep much better these days.

And I shouldn't be drinking coffee,
But a little bit won't hurt

So I pour enough to fill my cup halfway
And fill the rest with hot water

In my dream you were much taller
Not that I mind how you are now
Just for whatever reason, anyway

You were taller but it didn't seem abnormal
Like if it were real life it would have been abnormal
But ya know how in dreams everything just feels normal?
It was a lot like that

You were carrying me in your arms down a quiet road
Where down one side dried daffodils struggled to grow
Along the dusty embankment

And it was light out but there wasn't any sun
Just blue skied punctuated by tufts of white

There's this movie where the desert has

Twin suns and it's a bit like that
but in the opposite direction

Barren sprawl of shapeless land
Expanse of dead grass somehow
Still standing lifeless

A single tree in the sea of grayed blades
Where color seemed to either be bleeding out
At the tips of its branches or returning
From the base of its roots

You were no longer carrying me
We were walking together
I held my hand out to you
You didn't seem to notice

You were looking at the tree
While I was looking at the daffodils.

Finally I felt your hand tugging at my arm
Pulling me into the gray mass

I pulled hard
Until I slipped from your hand and fell
Then there was weeping

You cradled me
I could see   between my legs
Trickle of blood began to color the gray
Ground beneath us

Began   to   spread

Until entire ground beneath us had
Regained its color

Tears glistened in your eyes
You looked at me and tried to speak
All I could hear was a delicate breeze
Like a whisper being exhaled

I looked again at the daffodils
While everything was regaining its color
They were still wilted

Petals of the flowers began to
Fall away until only their innards
Remained skeletal and barren

A monument to their departed beauty.

When I looked at the tree it was still gray
At the ends of its branches

From behind it twin suns began to rise
And with it two infantile cries

A hand on my shoulder as I sat drinking coffee
At the kitchen table.
When I looked up it was you, a small smile
Looking down at me with happy eyes.

You shouldn't be drinking coffee…
A kiss on my head.

I know.

You poured yourself a cup.

Thank you for making the pot. I love you.

The tree's
color was returning.

I love you too.

About the Author

Brian R. Strauss is the author of *Call of the Void* , *Strung Like Puppets,* and *Existential Cowboy.* Raised in Chula Vista since 1993–he resides in San Diego with his partner and two cats.

www.ingramcontent.com/pod-product-compliance
Lightning Source LLC
Chambersburg PA
CBHW031337060726
47590CB00007B/2506
9780996322140